History: Scotland: St Andrew

560 Columba brings [...]

731-70[...] [...]ndrew

843-860 Scotland u[...]
1057-1093 King Malcolm Canmore. His wife, Margaret, introduces the Church of Rome to Scotland
    1127 Burgh of St Andrews founded
    1144 Church of St Rule completed
    1161-1318 St Andrews Cathedral built
    1200s St Andrews Castle built
    1310 Crail made a Royal Burgh
1314 Battle of Bannockburn. Robert the Bruce defeats English in War of Independence
    1411 University of St Andrews founded
    1450 Bishop Kennedy founded St Salvator's College
    1458 Falkland made a Royal Burgh
    1512 St Leonard's College founded
    1538 St Mary's College founded
    1539-1542 Palace of Falkland built by James V
1542-1567 Reign of Mary Queen of Scots
    1546 Murder of Cardinal Beaton
    1547 Siege of St Andrews Castle
    1552 Archbishop Hamilton guarantees St Andrews residents right to play golf on the links
    1559 St Andrews Cathedral sacked by Reformers
1560 Reformation: Scotland declared a Protestant country
    1587 Anstruther made a Royal Burgh
1603 Union of the Crowns of Scotland and England under James I & VI
1639-1651 Civil War
    1655 St Andrews Pier destroyed in storm
    1679 Archbishop Sharp murdered
1707 Union of Parliaments of Scotland and England
1715 & 1745 Jacobite rebellions
1750-1800 Age of Enlightenment in Scotland
    1754 The Society of St Andrews Golfers formed
    1833 Madras College school founded
1860 First Open Golf Championship held at Prestwick
    1834 The Royal and Ancient Golf Club founded
    1850 The railway reaches St Andrews
    1877 St Leonard's Girls School founded
    1889 Botanic Gardens founded in St Andrews
    1892 First women admitted to the University
    1897 Dundee University College affiliated to St Andrews University
    1960 Botanic Garden moved to its present site
    1967 Dundee and St Andrews Universities separated

History of St Andrews: The Town

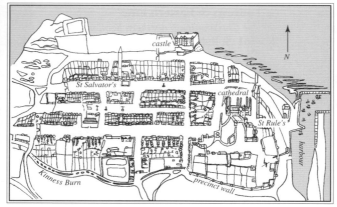

The town of St Andrews in the 16th century

It is not certain exactly when the first settlement was established on the present site of St Andrews, but it is recorded that under the Pictish kings in the 700s St Andrews, then called Kilrimont, was the capital of the region of the Pictish lands called *Fib* (later Fife). It was not until the twelfth century, however, that Bishop Robert founded the burgh, with the blessing of King David I. The early town was situated at the east end of North Street around the original castle.

By 1260 North Street, Market Street and South Street were laid out as they are today (though not extending so far), and by 1560 the town had spread to the West Port. St Andrews was not a walled town, as far as we know, but it did have four main gateways, of which the West Port is the only one remaining. South Street was the grand avenue leading to the gates of the Cathedral, North Street gave access to the bishops' burgh around the castle, and Market Street was the commercial area with the Tolbooth at the centre where the Whyte-Melville Memorial Fountain now stands.

The West Port

The first houses were wooden, but by the 1400s the burghers were erecting substantial stone houses facing the street. Each had a strip of land at the rear called a rigg, where animals were kept and vegetables grown. In later years many of the riggs were built over in order to house the growing population.

The town flourished throughout the Middle Ages until the Reformation in 1560. It was run by the burghers and the guilds of the many tradesmen working on the Cathedral. People came to see the relics of St Andrews and to study at the renowned university. During the 17th century a series of conflicts raged throughout Scotland, centred on the continuing power struggle between Presbyterians and Episcopalians. The fortunes of St Andrews during this period rose and fell with those of its resident bishops. In 1689 Presbyterianism finally became an established religion in Scotland and the Episcopacy was abolished. Consequently both the town and the University lost status. At the same time trade with Europe through the Fife

History (continued)

ports declined due to a series of wars with France and the opeinings up of trade with the Americas. Eye witnesses of the time commented on St Andrews' delapidated state.

Towards the end of the 1700s things began to improve as people started to recognise the town with its wonderful beaches, clean air and fine golf links as a suitable place for holidays or retirement. It was also the Age of Enlightenment in Scotland and many famous people visited the town – Dr Johnson in 1774; Sir Walter Scott in 1793 and again in 1827. But it was not until Major Sir Hugh Playfair, a retired officer, came to live in St Andrews in 1834, and subsequently became Provost, that the town was transformed into a thriving modern burgh. This was not easy, as the citizens were reluctant to embrace change, but with the help of like-minded individuals – such as Dr Adamson, who overhauled the town's sanitary arrangements – improvements were made. The burgh expanded into the New Town, at the western end of the town. Hotels were built, and the arrival of the railway in 1850 provided a big boost to the tourist trade.

The twentieth century has seen St Andrews grow in size and prosperity, with the expansion of the University and the growth of the golf industry. At the same time, it has retained much of its unique historic charm.

History of St Andrews: The Church

THE FIRST RECORD of Christianity at St Andrews (or Kilrimont as it was then known) is of the death of an Abbott in 743. His community were descendants of the Celtic church of St Columba. At about the same time legend has it that St Rule (or Regulus) was shipwrecked in St Andrews Bay when carrying relics (bones) of St Andrew the Apostle from Patras in Greece. He was granted land in Kilrimont by the Pictish King Angus I (729-761) to build a shrine.

In the 10th century the first Bishop was installed in Kilrimont by Constantine II, King of Alba (he was a grandson of Kenneth McAlpine who had united the Scots and the Picts in 843). By this time the relics of St Andrew were becoming objects of pilgrimage.

In the 11th century there were two important events which were greatly to influence the future of Kilrimont. First, St Rule's Tower and Church was built to house the relics of St Andrew, and second, the Norman Bishops were introduced to Scotland by Queen Margaret.

St Rule's Tower

Margaret, a Princess of King Alfred's house, fled the Norman invasion of England and arrived in Scotland in 1068. She married Malcolm Canmore, King of the Scots, and, devout Christian that she was, set about reorganising the church in Scotland on Roman lines. Bishop Turgot, her biographer, was the first of a long line of remarkable Norman bishops, and the first to use 'St Andrews' in his title. At this time St Andrews was said to be the largest and wealthiest see in Scotland.

St Andrews grew to be the centre of religious life in Scotland; a position it held until the reformation in 1560. Bishop Robert (early 12th century) extended St Rule's Church and brought the Augustinians to set up a priory; his successor, Arnold, began the building of the Cathedral

History (continued)

(eventually consecrated in 1318); and Bishop Roger built the first castle, to house the Bishop and his retinue in proper style.

In 1472 the Bishops became Archbishops, and in 1541 David Beaton was appointed the first Cardinal in Scotland. By this time the Church was very wealthy and powerful, but also – as throughout Europe – very corrupt.

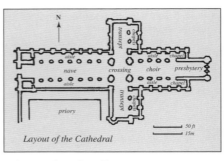

Layout of the Cathedral

In the 1500s news of the Protestant Reformation in Europe was brought to St Andrews by Patrick Hamilton, George Wishart and others. They were tried in the Cathedral and burnt at the stake for their beliefs. Wishart's death in 1546 was revenged three months later by his local supporters, who murdered Cardinal Beaton and occupied the Castle. A year-long siege ensued before Government forces retook the Castle.

In 1560 Catholicism was swept away and Protestantism was established in Scotland. Hamilton, the reigning Archbishop, was allowed to retain his title, but no public masses could be celebrated and he had no authority. He was executed in 1572, for allegedly plotting to murder the Regent. The Cathedral and Castle were abandoned and quickly fell into decay as their stonework was removed for other purposes.

For the next 100 years Scotland was riven by the battle between Presbyterianism and Episcopacy. Catholicism was not an issue, although many considered the Episcopalians to have papist leanings. The controversy was fuelled by the Monarchs of the time who believed in the divine right of Kings to govern, and wished to stamp their authority on the Church through the appointment of Bishops and control of forms of worship. During this time the centre of religious activity moved to Edinburgh and Glasgow, but during the two periods of Episcopacy (1606-38, 1661-89), St Andrews briefly prospered again.

During the 17th century a number of residents of St Andrews and Fife played leading roles in Scotland's religious struggles. Andrew Melville, first principal St Mary's College, was a leader in the formation of the Presbyterain church; James Graham, Marquis of Montrose, was a student at St Andrews (1627-1629) and a general of both Presbyterian and Royalist forces during the period; James Sharp was a minister of Crail who become Archbishop of St Andrews and was consequently murdered in 1679; and Richard Cameron, student of St Andrews and resident of Falkland, joined the Presbyterian Covenanters in their fight to worship as they wished and died in battle in 1680 (the Cameronian regiment was named after him).

The accession of William and Mary in 1689 marked the end of Bishops in Scotland until 1842, when the Episcopal Bishopric of St Andrews was restored (the title also includes Dunkeld and Dunblane). In 1878 a Catholic Archbishop of St Andrews and Edinburgh was appointed. Neither Bishop is based in St Andrews.

Presbyterianism was now established in Scotland and there were no further wars over the matter, but the next 200 years were dogged by the controversy over patronage (whether the church members or the gentry should appoint local ministers). Eventually, in 1843, the Church split and Thomas Chalmers, born in Anstruther and earlier Principal of St Mary's

History (continued)

theological college, became the first Moderator of the Free Church of Scotland. Patronage was eventually abolished in 1874, but the two branches of the Church did not reunite until 1929. Even then a small rump remained as the 'Wee Frees'.

History of St Andrews: The University

S COTTISH STUDENTS in the early Middle Ages travelled to England or the Continent to study, but by the early 1400s wars had made travel more difficult. St Andrews was already a centre for learning as well as religion, and Bishop Wardlaw and the Prior were keen to found Scotland's first university. They had the backing of the State, so, in 1410, they formed a group of graduates, all of whom were also clerics, and applied to the Pope for a charter. In February 1414, to great rejoicing in the town, the Charter arrived.

St Salvator's

The Charter gave authority for faculties of Theology, Law, Arts and Medicine to be established, and for the right to confer degrees. An elected Rector was to be in charge, and a Chancellor would retain a supervisory role (it remained the prerogative of the Archbishop to hold this post until the final abolition of the Episcopacy in 1689). In 1424 James I suggested that the University would be better sited in Perth, where it would be more central and freer from domination by the Church. The Pope did not agree and the King withdrew his proposal.

The first College was St John's (no longer in existence), which lay to the west of the Parliament Hall. There were also independent teachers, called Regents, who competed for students. The Regents were difficult to control and were finally abolished in 1747. In 1450 Bishop Kennedy founded the college of St Salvator, the original chapel and tower of which still stand. This was a residential College and students began their studies at the age of about 13.

In 1512 St Leonard's College, for poor clerks, was founded by Prior Hepburn. Most were novices and the rules were very strict. The college was situated within the Priory wall, next to St Leonard's Chapel. The last college, St Mary's, was founded in 1538 by Archbishop Beaton in an attempt to improve the education of the secular clergy. It incorporated the original college of St John's.

During its first 150 years the University thrived. It was well financed by the Church and attracted prestigious teachers from all over Europe. Many of the leading figures in Scotland studied there.

The Reformation in 1560 caused confusion, but the government of the day decreed that the universities should continue and that St Andrews should have preference. From that time on, however, the State increasingly took control from the Church. Andrew Melville, the great Protestant reformer, became principal of St Mary's College in 1580. He brought order to the University but was banished when the Bishops were restored in 1606. Thereafter, until 1689, the fortunes of the University fluctuated depending on whether or not there was a Bishop in residence, but according to reports of the day students were able to follow their studies in relative peace.

History (continued)

Famous characters of this period include James Graham, Marquis of Montrose, who was a student from 1627-29; Sir John Scot of Scotstarvit, who founded a chair of Latin at St Leonard's College in 1620; and Archbishop Sharp, ex officio Chancellor from 1661-79, who ruled the University as strictly as his Presbyterian predecessor Andrew Melville, and is remembered for the Regius Professorship of Mathematics in 1668.

Following the loss of the Bishops in 1689 St Andrews became a relative backwater, and throughout the following century the University experienced a period of decline. It no longer received special treatment from the Government and, with the exception of St Leonard's, the colleges were inadequately endowed. The intake of students became much more localised and numbers dropped as low as 150. St Salvator's and St Leonard's amalgamated in 1747 to form the United College, largely to consolidate finances, but despite this the buildings fell into serious disrepair. This period saw the end of the collegiate system, with students preferring to live in lodgings (later known as 'bunks') and the academic staff no longer willing to undertake supervision of residences.

In 1697 the Marquis of Breadalbane was appointed chancellor (he later became Duke of Atholl and Secretary of Scotland). Like James I before him, he recommended that the University should be moved to a more accessible part of the country. Plans were drawn up and land was allocated on the south side of Perth by the River Tay, but the project was dropped following disagreement about the details.

The 1800s saw a continual succession of Commissions. It was an anxious time for the University. Under the direction of the commissioners, buildings were repaired and new ones built – the most important being the United College quadrangle (1829-46). In addition, the administration was reorganised, with a senior executive Principal being appointed to administer the University and the Rectorship reduced to an honorary position. By the end of the century student numbers had increased to 500 and the University was once again attracting staff of the highest quality.

In 1896 a women's residence, University Hall, was built on the western edge of the town. In 1877 a scheme was instituted which allowed women to enter for examinations. This scheme looked forward to the admission of women to full membership of the University in 1892.

Through the 20th century St Andrews was dominated by three Principals: Irvine 1921 -1952, Knox 1953-1966 and Watson 1966-1986. Irvine had been educated at St Andrews and subsequently became professor of Chemistry. He was a controversial figure who had visions of resurrecting the collegiate system. He had St Salvator's Hall built next to the United College with that in mind (first opened in 1930 and completed in 1940).

Knox, Professor of Moral Philosophy, was also a St Andrews man. He wanted the University to be small, centralised and of high quality, concentrating on academic subjects. He was disappointed

St Leonard's Chapel

History (continued)

that the town would not agree to new building adjacent to the old and he had to accept the North Haugh on the edge of town as the site for the new science buildings, begun in 1964.

Both Principals were dogged by problems over University College Dundee. Formed in 1883 and affiliated to St Andrews in 1897, the college felt, with some justification, discriminated against. The Tedder Commission (1951–3) formed Queen's College, Dundee and advised that it should concentrate on technical and professional subjects and St Andrews on academic ones. In practice this curtailed the development of St Andrews, and by 1959 Dundee was the swifter-growing of the two institutions. In 1967 they split into two separate universities.

Principal Watson was unconnected with St Andrews prior to his appointment. Perhaps this made it easier for him to steer the University successfully through a period of very rapid expansion (encouraged by the Government) during the sixties and seventies, and a subsequent retrenchment in the eighties. The University is now entering the new millennium in good shape, with an impressive number of new buildings and a complement of about 6000 students.

St Andrews retains some of its ancient traditions. Some first year students, or 'bejants', undergo an initiation ceremony on 'Raisin Monday'. The students' highly visible red gowns, said to date from the 1700s, were originally worn in order to prevent them from 'vaging *[wandering]* and vice'. The Kate Kennedy Pageant is more recent, dating from the last century (Kate was the niece of Bishop Kennedy, the founder of St Salvator's College). It remains a lively occasion and is a popular sight for tourists.

St Mary's College

After the Sunday service at the University Chapel the students process to the end of the pier wearing their red gowns, possibly in memory of John Honey – a student who, in 1800, rescued eight sailors from a wreck off the East Sands single-handed.

History of St Andrews: Golf

For many people, the town of St Andrews is primarily known for its golf courses. Golf was played in Scotland from the early 1400s, but the first written reference to the game dates from 1457, when James II decreed that golf and 'futeball' should not be played as it kept men away from their archery practice. In a similar way, kirk sessions in the following century opposed golf because it kept men from going to church.

The first reference to

The Royal & Ancient Golf Club

History (continued)

golf in St Andrews dates from 1552, when Archbishop Hamilton guaranteed the rights of St Andreans to play golf, together with other sports, on the now famous Links (they remain public property to this day). Golfing was free of charge for all until 1913, and for local rate payers until 1946 when an annual subscription was introduced. There are now six courses (one nine hole), run by the St Andrews Links Trust and its Management Committee, and even the Old Course – the course used for the Open and other major events – can be played by the general public.

The Swilken Bridge on the Old Course

Golf grew to be a popular sport. James Melville refers in his diaries to the pleasures of playing golf as a student in the 1500s, while the Marquis of Montrose (at St Andrews from 1627-29) also enjoyed the sport. By 1691 St Andrews was being referred to as the 'Metropolis of Golfing'.

In 1754 twenty-two local noblemen and gentry formed the Society of St Andrews Golfers, which obtained royal patronage in 1834 when King William IV granted the society the title 'The Royal and Ancient Golf Club of St Andrews'. In 1854 they built the Royal and Ancient Club House, which remains a landmark to this day, and in 1873 the first Open Championship was played in St Andrews. In 1897 the R & A was asked to draw up the standard rules for the increasingly popular sport. These are now used by clubs throughout the world. In 1968 the Willie Auchterlonie Golf Museum was opened and also the Old Golf Course Hotel, which accommodates some of the many visitors flocking to the Mecca of Golf.

Many famous people come to St Andrews to play. President Eisenhower played the course in 1946. There were also the famous American golfers: Bobby Jones, who was made a freeman of the town in 1958, and Jack Nicklaus, who received an honorary degree from the University in 1984. They both fell in love with St Andrews and played in and won many competitions.

Not to be forgotten are the famous golfing residents of St Andrews. Tom Morris and his son Young Tom, who won the Open four times in a row but sadly died in 1875 at only 24 (he is buried in the precinct together with his wife, who died shortly before him). Also Willie Auchterlonie, who won the Open in 1893.

> Old Tom Morris 1821-1908
> Open Champion
> 1861, 1862, 1864 and 1867
> Born in a house which stood on this site
> 16th June 1821

See *Walk 1*

The game of golf has changed over the years. In 1618 a 'featherie' ball was used (goose feathers packed into a leather bag). The longest drive with such a ball was reputedly 360 yards in 1836. These balls were time-consuming to make and did not last long and were succeeded in the late 1840s by 'gutta percha' balls. These were not entirely satisfactory, and eventually the present day rubbercored balls took their place in 1899. Clubs were of hickory until the twentieth century, when steel shafted clubs were introduced. Both clubs and balls were, and still are, produced in St Andrews. J Petts is known to have supplied the Marquis of Montrose with clubs in 1672, and there have been many other makers in the town, including Robert Forgan, in the early 1800s, and the Auchterlonie family, who are still in business today.

Walk 1: *Old Course & New Town*

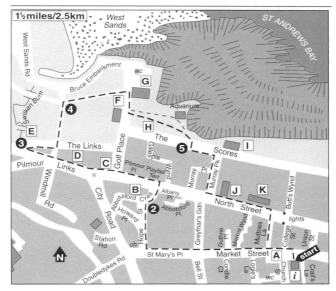

Start at the Tourist Information Centre in Market Street. Cross the street and turn left, passing the G J Whyte-Melville Memorial Fountain (A) on your left, then continue along Market Street and then St Mary's Place. Just before Hope Park Church (spire) turn right along Howard Place/Hope Street. Go as far as Abbotsford Crescent (B), leaving Howard Place on your left.

2 Turn right and follow the Crescent down to Playfair Terrace/ Pilmour Place. Cross the road and turn left. Cross the end of Golf Place and continue along Pilmour Links past Auchterlonies Shop (C) and Rusacks Hotel (D) to the end of the road.

3 Turn sharp right along The Links, passing the Swilken Bridge (E) on the 18th fairway of the Old Course, on your left. Turn left along a wide tarred path crossing the fairway with the Royal and Ancient Golf Club (F) up to the right. If you wish to break off from this walk to see more of the Course turn left at this point, passing the broad beach of the West Sands, backed by dunes, to your right.

4 To continue this route, turn first right and follow the path up to the Bristish Golf Museum (G). Cross the road and turn right then almost immediately take the metalled path to the left, signposted to the Castle and Visitor Centre (*see* Walk 2). Climb up past the Martyrs' Monument (H) on your right. (At this point you can make a detour to the left to visit the Aquarium).

5 When you reach the road – The Scores – carry on till just before St James Roman Catholic Church (I) then cross the road and turn right up Murray Park. At the top of the road, turn left into North Street passing the birthplace of Tom Morris (J), and continuing past the New Cinema and the Crawford Arts Centre (K). Cross the street and go down Muttoes Lane which leads you back into Market Street. Turn left and cross the street to return to the Tourist Information Centre.

Walk 1 (continued)

A **Whyte-Melville Memorial Fountain:** This was once the site of the Tolbooth (town hall) and Mercat Cross (demolished in 1862 and 1768 respectively). The monument (1880) is to a local writer.

Memorial Fountain

B **Abbotsford Crescent:** Built in 1865 by John Chesser in classical style. Part of the Crescent was home of Professor McIntosh who bequeathed it to the University as a Hall of Residence (McIntosh Hall) in 1931.

C **Auchterlonies Shop:** Named after Willie Auchterlonie (Open Golf Champion 1893). He was Honorary Professional of the Royal and Ancient Golf Club from 1935-1963. His son, Laurie, also a skilled golf club maker, succeeded him as Honorary Professional. He died in 1987.

D **Rusacks Hotel:** Built and opened in 1887 by John Wilhelm Christ of Rusack, a German who came to Britain in 1871. He owned several hotels in St Andrews before building Rusacks. The hotel became famous and has been patronised by Royalty and many celebreties in the Golfing World.

E **Swilken Bridge:** A pack horse bridge, built in the Middle Ages on the route north from St Andrews. Now a landmark on the Old Course.

Rusacks Hotel

F **The Royal and Ancient Golf Club:** Built in 1854. In 1754, 22 noblemen of Fife formed the Society of St Andrews Golfers. In 1834 King William IV became patron of what then became The Royal and Ancient Golf Club. It remains a private club with a membership of 1800. Since 1897 the R & A has been recognised as 'the Governing Authority for the Rules of Golf in all countries except the USA, Canada and Mexico'.

British Golf Museum

G **British Golf Museum:** Built in 1990, partially funded by the R & A.

H **Martyrs' Monument:** Erected in 1842 in memory of protestant martyrs burnt at the stake in St Andrews in the 16th century.

I **St James Church:** Roman Catholic, built in 1910. This church took the place of the *Tin Tabernacle* erected in 1885. At the time of the Reformation the clergy became Protestant and there was no resident Catholic priest in St Andrews until 1884.

Martyrs' Monument

J **Tom Morris:** Old Tom Morris (1821-1908) was born and lived in North Street. A golf celebrity, he was appointed Keeper of the Greens of the R & A in 1865 (the 18th hole of the Old Course, which he laid out, is named in his memory). He started playing golf at the age of 6, and won the Open Championship four times. His son, Young Tom, a brilliant golfer, also won the Open four times but sadly died when he was 24.

K **The Crawford Arts Centre:** Adam style house built in about 1812. Originally built as a town house, it became a preparatory school in 1824. In 1978 the building was sold and developed as an Arts Centre.

Walk 2: *Castle, Harbour & Cathedral*

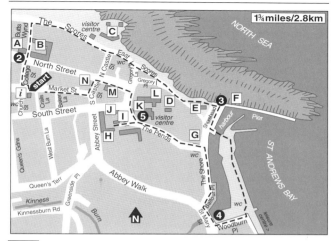

Start at the Tourist Information Centre. Cross Market Street, turn left and immediately right into College Street; continue to North Street, immediately opposite you is Butts Wynd with the Old Student Union Building (A) ahead and to the left, and St Salvator's Tower and the University Chapel (both B) to the right with the Quadrangle behind. All well worth a visit.

2 Go down Butts Wynd and turn right along The Scores, continue past the Castle (C) on the left with its Visitor Centre. Walk on with the sea on the left until you reach the Precinct Wall (D) of the Cathedral (ignore this entrance to the Cathedral, you pass the main entrance later on the route). Continue (now on a tarred path) by the Wall towards the harbour. When the path splits, go left passing the ruins of St Mary on the Rock (E) on the way. Continue down to the harbour with its historic Pier (F).

3 At the bottom of the hill turn right along the harbour front, then left over the footbridge between the inner and outer harbour, and follow the path between the beach and a putting green until you reach a road cutting off to the right. Turn right and follow this to the junction with St Mary Street.

4 Turn right, cross the Kinness Burn and almost immediately turn right along Balfour Place into The Shore with the Precinct Wall on your left. When the Wall ends, turn left through the Sea Yett or gate (G) and walk up the Pends. At the top of the Pends pass through the Nun's Gate into St Leonard's School (H). St Leonard's Chapel (I) is immediately on your right with Queen Mary's House (J) behind.

5 Retrace your steps to the Pends and swing left through the Pends Gateway (K) and continue straight ahead. The main entrance to the Cathedral (L) is on your right (this might be a good time to explore the Cathedral and climb St Rule's Tower which has a commanding view). Turn left along North Street, passing the Preservation Trust Museum (M) on your left. Turn left into South Castle Street (N) continue to Market Street, cross the road, turn right and go the short distance back to the Tourist Information Centre.

Walk 2 (continued)

A **Old Student Union Building:** Probably built in 15th century but altered in the 18th. Said to have been the home of the '*Admirable*' James Crichton (1560-1582) when a student. He mastered 10 languages and was talented in all walks of life. He was murdered, aged 21, while working for the Duke of Mantua in Italy. From 1892 to 1963 the building housed the Men's Student Union. It is now a coffee shop.

B **St Salvator's Tower and Chapel:** All that is left of the oldest college of the University, it was built in 1450-1460 by Bishop James Kennedy (d. 1465), who founded the University in 1411. The Tower with its spire is the highest in St Andrews, it was used as a gun emplacement to besiege the castle in 1547. Above the gateway can be seen the coat of arms of Bishop Kennedy. Set in the pavement outside the gateway are the initials PH marking the spot where Patrick Hamilton was burnt at the stake.

St Salvator's Chapel

Chapel: Access is from the Quadrangle, go through the arch and turn right. Only the nave and apse remain. The chapel ceased to be a place of worship between 1560 and 1760, being used as the meeting place of the Commissary Court of St Andrews from 1563. From 1761-1904 it housed the congregation of St Leonard's parish. The main item of interest is the tomb of Bishop Kennedy, founder of the University. He designed it himself. Sunday morning service is attended here by the students wearing their red gowns.

Quadrangle: Built during the 19th century, including the flying buttresses along the chapel wall, it is on the original site of Bishop Kennedy's St Salvator's College.

C **Castle:** There was a castle on this site from the end of the 12th century but most of the present Castle was built by Bishop Trail at the end of the 14th century. The Castle was the Bishops' palace, but also a fortress and a prison. In 1546 Cardinal David Beaton burnt George Wishart at the stake outside the castle. Wishart's

The Castle

Protestant supporters captured the Castle and murdered Beaton. They in turn were besieged, John Knox being amongst those who came to support them. Despite efforts by the besiegers to dig a tunnel into the Castle the Protestants held out till the French Fleet appeared in the bay. Archbishop John Hamilton restored the castle and improved the accommodation, but he was hanged in 1571. After the Reformation the castle fell into disrepair and in 1603 it was separated from the church and given to the Earl of Dunbar. The bottle dungeon and the tunnel are of particular interest.

D **Precinct Wall:** This wall surrounded the Cathedral and Priory. It was half a mile long and twenty feet high. Thirteen towers and four gateways still survive. Originally built in the 14th century, parts of the wall are known to have been rebuilt in the early 1500s by Prior Hepburn. One of the towers is alleged to be haunted by a white lady.

E **St Mary on the Rock:** Ruin of a 12th-century church, on the site of an earlier Culdean church. The Culdees were the first Christians to come to St Andrews. They were the keepers of the sacred relics of St Andrew but were later sidelined by the Augustinians and died out by the 14th Century.

Walk 2 (continued)

F **Harbour and Pier:** The original wooden pier was destroyed in 1655 by a storm, and was rebuilt in the following year with stone from the cathedral. The students make a ritual walk to the end of the pier after Sunday service in the University Chapel. St. Andrews was a thriving fishing and trading port up to 1925.

The Harbour & Pier

G **The Sea Yett:** 16th-century gate giving access to the Priory from the harbour.

H **St Leonard's School:** Formerly the site of St Leonard's College, the girls' boarding and day school (founded in 1877) moved here in 1882.

I **St Leonard's Chapel:** Originally 15th-century, it was reconstructed in 1512 when it became part of the College of St Leonard's. The college was united with St Salvator's in 1747 to form the United College, and the buildings were sold. The chapel was reroofed in 1910 and extensively renovated in 1948-1952. There is public access.

J **Queen Mary's House:** Built by Hugh Scrymgeour, a local merchant, in 1520. Mary Queen of Scots stayed here in 1562. It now houses St Leonard's School library. It is not open to the public.

K **The Pends and Pends Gateway:** The gateway at the top of the Pends (passage) was built around 1350 and was the main entrance to the Precinct.

L **Cathedral:** Started in 1161 by Bishop Arnold, as St Rule's church was already thought to be too small, the Cathedral was finished in 1318 by Bishop Lamberton. Robert the Bruce was at the consecration. The west gable blew down in 1270 and the western front had to be rebuilt after a fire in 1378. The architecture reflects both the Romanesque and Gothic styles, and at 357ft long it was the largest cathedral in Scotland. In 1559 the Cathedral was sacked by the people of the town after a sermon by John Knox in Holy Trinity Church. After the Reformation the Cathedral soon fell into disrepair and was used as a stone quarry.

The Cathedral

Priory: The Augustinians were brought to St Andrews in 1144 by Bishop Robert to administer the cathedral church of St Rule's, and the Priory was built in the 13th century. Only the foundations remain, but there is a visitor centre which houses many of the ancient stone remains.

St Rule's Tower: The last remains of St Rule's Church, built in the 11th and 12th centuries. It is thought to have been one of the largest churches of its time in Scotland. The tower is 108 feet high. The present ruins are thought to have been built on the site of an older church which housed the relics of St Andrew. Tickets for access to the Tower can be obtained from the Cathedral Visitor Centre.

M **Preservation Trust Museum:** Originally a fisherman's cottage, the museum (open from 2pm to 5pm in the summer) recreates the history of the town. The Trust's aim is to preserve historic St Andrews.

N **South Castle Street:** Contains fine examples of forestairs, pantiles, crowstepped gables and other aspects of traditional architecture.

Walk 3: *Kinness Burn & Botanics*

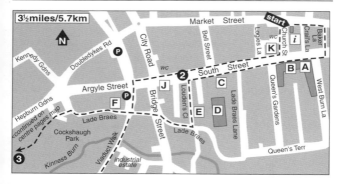

Start at the Tourist Information Centre, turn right up Market Street and take the second turning on the right down Baker Lane. Cross South Street and turn right along the wall of Parliament Hall (A) – the entry to St Mary's College (B) is on your left. Cross Queen's Gardens and then Lade Braes Lane. On the left beyond is the ruin of Blackfriars Chapel (C) with Madras College (D) set back behind it.

② Turn left down Louden's Close (E), and right along Lade Braes (F). Cross Bridge Street, and continue along the path opposite until you reach Cockshaugh Park. Walk along the northern side of the park, at the end you can take either the upper or the lower path (*see* centre pages map).

Louden's Close

③ At the next junction (you can turn left across the burn and up the hill to the Canongate, a useful shortcut) branch right, through a barrier, and then left past an old cottage. You are now entering a conservation area. Continue through woodland, at the end of the second open space you pass a small bridge on your left. Shortly after, turn left over a little humpbacked bridge and climb up a tarmac path to a pond. Law Mill (G) now in ruins is to the left of it. Continue past the pond taking the second turning right (signposted) to view a recently restored Doocot (H) in a small housing estate.

④ Retrace your steps and continue on the original path to the main road, the Canongate. Turn left and walk for about 15 minutes to arrive at the Botanic Garden (I) on your left, a very pleasant place to stop for a while.

The Doocot

⑤ Leave the Garden and continue along the Canongate looking out for Viaduct Walk cutting off to the left. Follow this as it crosses Lade Braes, pass through the car park beyond to Argyle Street. Turn right and you will see the West Port (J) in front of you. Go through it and walk along the left-hand side of South Street past Holy Trinity Church (K). Turn left down Church Street and right into Market Street. The Tourist Information Centre is ahead on the right.

Walk 3 (continued)

A University Library/Parliament Hall: First completed in 1643 as the University Library, the building gained its secondary name after the Scottish Parliament sat here from November 1645 to February 1646.

B St Mary's College: Founded 1538 by Archbishop James Beaton for the purpose of educating the clergy better so that they could combat the growing Protestant heresy. Ironically its most famous principal, Andrew Melville 1580, was a great leader of the Reformed Church. The Stair Tower, home of the Divinity Faculty and the Principal's House, is on the west side of the quadrangle and dates from the 16th century. The holm oak in the centre of the quad was planted in 1750 and the thorn bush at the entrance to the Stair Tower replaced one reputed to have been planted by Mary Queen of Scots in 1560.

C Blackfriars Chapel: Ruined remains of a church built by the Dominicans who came to St Andrews in the 13th century. They were driven out at the time of the Reformation.

D Madras College: Opened in 1833, the college was founded with money donated by the Rev Andrew Bell who had been a missionary in India. He developed a system where the senior pupils taught the younger ones which proved effective and economical and became quite widespread in Scotland. Madras is now the secondary school for the area.

Blackfriars Chapel

E Louden's Close: One of the finest survivng examples of a medieval wynd.

F Lade Braes: Until the 19th century this was the southern boundary of the town. Some of the existing walls date back to the 16th century.

G Law Mill: The most famous of several mills in the town. Probably built in the 13th century, it originally belonged to the Priory, but had been taken over by the Burgh by 1660.

H Doocot: Restored by the Preservation Trust, this also belonged to the Priory and the pigeons provided a good supply of fresh meat.

I Botanic Garden: The original garden was founded in St Mary's College in 1889 but was moved to its present location in 1960. The plants are well labelled with a large show of azaleas and rhododendrons. Well worth a visit.

J West Port: The only remaining ancient gateway into the burgh, it was rebuilt in 1589 and there have been further alterations since then. On the west facing wall is a panel showing David I, inserted in 1843.

K Holy Trinity Church: This building was begun in 1411 but all that remains of the original structure is the tower. The rest of the church was rebuilt in 1907. John Knox preached here in 1559 and incited the congregation to loot the church and the cathedral. The church is not generally open to the public.

Holy Trinity Church

Contents

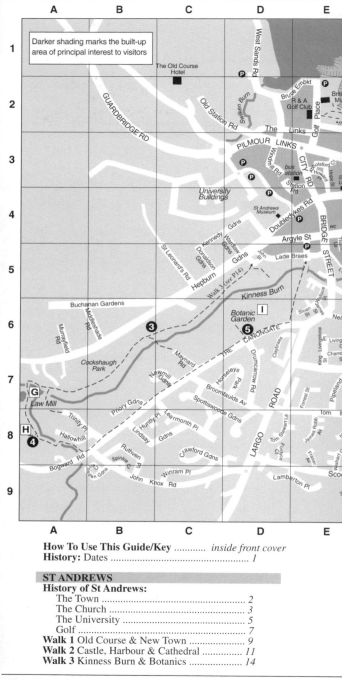

How To Use This Guide/Key	*inside front cover*
History: Dates	*1*

ST ANDREWS
History of St Andrews:
The Town	*2*
The Church	*3*
The University	*5*
Golf	*7*
Walk 1 Old Course & New Town	*9*
Walk 2 Castle, Harbour & Cathedral	*11*
Walk 3 Kinness Burn & Botanics	*14*

Published by: Hallewell Publications, Port-an-Eilean, Strathtummel, Perthshire, PH16 5RU
Printed by: Woods of Perth Ltd, Perth

St Andrews Street Map

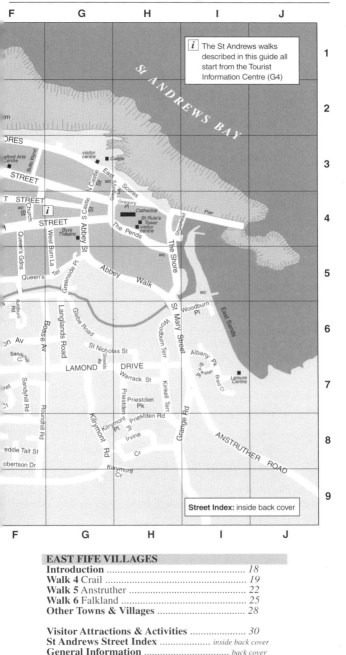

EAST FIFE VILLAGES
Introduction *18*
Walk 4 Crail *19*
Walk 5 Anstruther *22*
Walk 6 Falkland *25*
Other Towns & Villages *28*

Visitor Attractions & Activities *30*
St Andrews Street Index .... *inside back cover*
General Information .... *back cover*

While every care has been taken in the preparation of this guide, the publishers cannot accept responsibility for any loss, damage or injury resulting from its use.

East Fife Villages: Introduction

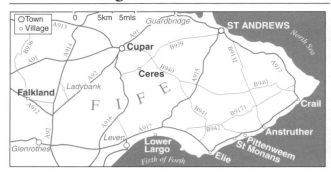

THE FOCUS OF MOST VISITS to East Fife is St Andrews, but that is not all there is to see. Trade, fishing, industry, agriculture and royal connections have all led to periods of local prosperity: a prosperity reflected – in Fife more than in any other area of Scotland – in the building of handsome towns and villages.

Sharps Close, Falkland (Walk 6)

In the following pages I have described walks round three of the most interesting villages in East Fife – **Crail**, **Anstruther** and **Falkland**. Following that I have listed six further settlements – the town of **Cupar** and the villages of **Pittenweem**, **St Monans**, **Elie**, **Lower Largo** and **Ceres** – which are also worth a visit.

A glance at the map will show that most of the villages are on the coast. These are harbour towns which originated in the medieval period. They are notable for their steep, narrow 'wynds' and tight-packed buildings rich in vernacular detail: orange pantiled roofs, crow-stepped gables and forestairs. You may also notice the occasional curved Dutch gable or other foreign influence: the result of the area's ancient trade with the Low Countries and the Baltic.

When this trade declined, the ports were predominantly used for fishing. The history of this industry can be explored at the splendid Scottish Fisheries Museum in Anstruther, while the modern industry survives principally in Pittenweem.

Inland, prosperity came through farming. Cupar was once both the County Town and Fife's main market town. Nearby Ceres includes the Folk Museum which contains exhibits relating to farming and other subjects of local importance.

School Wynd, Pittenweem

Falkland, tiny but very pretty, is of interest primarily because of its royal connections. The splendid Falkland Palace (open to the public) was a 16th-century royal hunting lodge: one of the finest Renaissance buildings in Scotland.

Public Transport: For local bus services, check with Tourist Information Centres.

Walk 4: *Crail*

The oldest and most prosperous of the East Neuk towns, Crail's attractions include its fine old parish church; the tolbooth, set in a spacious square; and the picturesque harbour at the bottom of a steep cobbled street.

food available; shops (general/specialist); wc

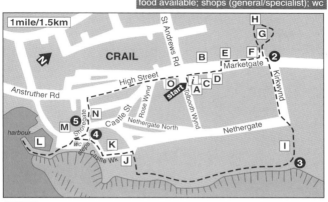

Start at the Museum and Heritage Centre (A), where the Tourist Information Centre is also situated. Turn right along Marketgate North (B), pass the Tolbooth (C) immediately on your right and continue past Andrew Mitchell's Fountain and then the Mercat Cross (D). Cross to the north side of the street. The Auld Hoose (E) is in front of you. Turn right, passing Kirkmay House (E), then left into the churchyard after a short distance. Immediately on your left is a huge boulder: The Blue Stone (F). The Parish Church (G) is in front of you. Walk round the back of the church and you will see in front of you the Dead House (H). Continue round the church and return to Marketgate.

2 Turn left along Marketgate, which narrows here. Cross the road and walk down Kirkwynd, signposted for the beach, which leads to the sea. Cross the end of the Nethergate on your right and continue on the path down the hill past the round, white Doocot (I) to the cliff top, which offers a wonderful view of the Isle of May. Down on the left is Roome Bay with its yellow sandy beach, safe for bathing.

3 Turn right along the shore path and follow it across a small burn, ignoring a footpath cutting off to the right (part of the Fife Coastal Path). There are excellent views of the Bass Rock and North Berwick Law in the distance. Carry on, until you see the Castle Wall ahead with its Victorian gazebo perched on the south-western corner. Follow the path as it swings right up a steep path with steps. At the top is the site of The King's Mill, of which only the Watch House remains (J). Turn left between the Castle Wall (K) and the Watch House into Castle Walk. Continue below the wall, turning right at the panoramic map and an old sundial. From this point you have your first view of the picturesque harbour below.

4 Descend some steps into Shoregate. There is no street name but you will see the harbour (L) ahead. Continue down the hill, with the white-harled Custom House (M) on the right. When you reach the

Walk 4 (continued)

water veer left and go to the end of the east pier, from where there is a lovely view looking back at the harbour and the town behind. Retrace your steps and go back up Shoregate (N).

❺ Pass Castle Street on your right (if you go up Castle Street you will see a sign directing you to the Pottery). Continue up the hill to the High Street. Turn right and continue in an easterly direction. Opposite St Andrews Road is the Golf Hotel (O), on your right. Cross Tolbooth Wynd and you are back at the Information Centre.

[A] **Museum and Heritage Centre:** Opened in 1979 by the Crail Preservation Society and housed in an 18th-century house, the museum includes an exhibition of local history.

[B] **Marketgate:** Site of markets since the early 1300s, when Crail was made a Royal Burgh. Market day was Sunday until 1560 when, following the Reformation, it was moved to Saturday. This was one of the largest market places in medieval Europe.

[C] **Tolbooth** (town hall/jail): The lower part of the tower was built in 1598 as a prison. The upper part of the tower you see today was built in 1776 to replace a wooden structure. It houses the bell and clock taken from the church. The bell was cast in Holland in 1520. The attached Town Hall was built in 1814.

The Tolbooth

[D] **Mercat Cross:** The shaft dates from the 17th century. It was moved to its present site in 1887.

[E] **Auld Hoose and Kirkmay House:** Two fine examples of the town's architecture, built in 1686 (probably Crail's oldest house) and 1817 respectively.

[F] **The Blue Stone:** Legend says that the Devil, in a fit of spite, threw the stone at the church from the Isle of May. The rock split, the other half landing on the beach to the east of the town.

Mercat Cross

The Blue Stone

[G] **The Parish Church:** Built in the late 12th century, with the tower added in the 13th century. The church was dedicated to the celtic Saint Maelrubha, from Wester Ross, by the Bishop of St Andrews. The name was later changed to St Mary. The church belonged to the Cistercian Nuns from Haddington, in East Lothian. In 1517 the church was upgraded to Collegiate status, with a provost and 10 prebendaries. The building was enlarged and acquired rich furnishings, but after John Knox preached here, in 1559, it was stripped of its riches. James Sharp was Presbyterian minister here from 1648-1660. He later turned Episcopalian and was made Archbishop of St

The Parish Church

Walk 4 (continued)

Andrews. In 1679 he was murdered on Magus Muir by Covenanters. The graveyard is full of interest, with most of the stones dating from the 17th century.

The church is open in the afternoon during the summer. There are guided tours and also a useful guide book.

H The Dead House (mortuary): Built in 1826, at the time when bodies were being illegally disinterred for medical research. Bodies were kept safe here for up to three months, by which time they were no longer suitable for dissection.

The Dead House

Doocot

I Doocot: Built in the 16th century (restored 1962). The pigeons were a source of fresh meat for the residents of the adjacent nunnery.

J King's Mill and Watch House: First built in the 12th century, all that remains of the mill is the Watch House. The mill fell into disuse in the 19th century, following a long history of dispute over its water supply.

K Castle Wall: The castle was built by David I in the 12th century and remained important up to the end of the 14th century. The castle had fallen into ruin by the early 18th century and is now the site of Crail House. Only parts of the old perimeter walls remain.

L Harbour: Crail was a flourishing port from the Middle Ages until the early 18th century, principally due to fishing and trade with Europe – particularly Holland. It was famous for its dried haddock, called a 'Crail Capon'. The curved east pier dates from the 16th century, while the west pier was built by Robert Stevenson, grandfather of the poet and novelist Robert Louis Stevenson, in 1826. Crail harbour is now a centre for lobster fishing.

The Harbour

Custom House

M Custom House: Built in the 17th century and restored in 1964 by the Crail Preservation Trust.

N Shoregate: The oldest road in the town, and the site of many well-preserved examples of domestic architecture from the 17th to the 19th centuries.

O Golf Hotel: Site of an inn since the 14th century. The present building dates from the 18th century. Crail Golfing Society, the 7th oldest club in the world, met here first in 1786. The golf course and club house are at Balcomie, about 2 miles/3km east of the town.

House in Shoregate

Walk 5: *Anstruther*

At one time the home to a large herring fleet and a centre for trade with the Low Countries, Anstruther was also a haven for smugglers. The town's main industry these days is tourism, centred on the Scottish Fisheries Museum by the still busy harbour.

food available; shops (general/specialist); wc

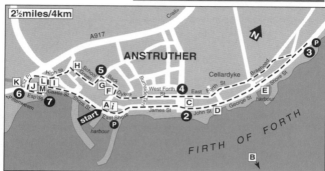

Start at the Tourist Information Centre. Immediately next door is the Scottish Fisheries Museum (A). It might be helpful to visit this before starting out on a stroll round the town. Tied up in the harbour opposite the Museum is the *Reaper*: a Fifie herring drifter. Turn left out of the Tourist Information Centre – the Lifeboat House is immediately opposite – and walk away from the town centre, passing one of the leading lights for the harbour on the way. Follow East Shore/East Green as it leads into James Street, with high old houses on both sides, and views of the Isle of May (B) through the wynds which run down to the sea. Continue to a T-junction with Tolbooth Wynd. The Cellardyke Town Hall (C) is straight in front of you.

❷ Turn right, then immediately left into John Street: a narrow street with one or two good examples of traditional architecture (D). Pass the harbour of Cellardyke (E) and continue along the street beyond, to the old outdoor bathing pool.

❸ It is possible to continue eastwards along the Fife Coastal Path towards Crail, but for this route retrace your steps to the start of the houses and strike diagonally up the hill on a narrow footpath heading back towards Anstruther, joining an unmetalled road with front gardens on the right and a wall on the left, through which you can catch glimpses of back gardens falling steeply to the houses below. If it is a clear day you should have a wonderful view across the Firth of Forth to the Bass Rock and North Berwick Law. When the path ends, continue along the tarred road, then on along East Forth Street. Cross Tolbooth Wynd into West Forth Street.

❹ Continue along West Forth Street. When it ends cross Burnside Terrace and continue along the tarmac path beyond with a playground on the right, then go along Back Dykes road. When you reach the end of the road, there is a large white house in front of you: Johnstone Lodge (F). At this point turn right up Chalmers Brae, then left into a continuation of Back Dykes. On the left behind the

Walk 5 (continued)

second high wall is Melville's Manse (G).

5 Follow the cobbled road, then turn first right (School Green). St Adrian's Parish Church (H) stands up on the right. At the far end of the churchyard turn left at a T-junction, go down the hill and turn right into the High Street. Continue along this, crossing the main road and passing Old Post Office Close (I) (birthplace of Thomas Chalmers) on your left. Continue to the junction with the main road to Crail. The road bends to the left and crosses the Dreel Burn before entering Elizabeth Place with the Anstruther Wester Church (J) on your left. As the High Street swings right the Ship Master's house is straight ahead and on the right-hand corner opposite is Buckie House (K).

6 Turn left and go down the Esplanade, with the Old Manse straight ahead. Continue down to the water's edge, where there is a good view of the harbour wall.

7 Retrace your steps, recrossing the Dreel Burn and turning into the High Street, then take the first turning right, down Wightmans Wynd (L). At the foot of the Wynd (Dreel House (M) is immediately on the right) turn left and continue along the cobbled street (Castle Street), and on into Shore Street. On the right is the Pier with Chalmer's Lighthouse at the end.

Continue along the sea front to return to the Tourist Office.

A **Scottish Fisheries Museum:** Officially opened in 1969, the museum covers all aspects of the Fishing Industry. It has a tearoom and is wheelchair-friendly.

The collection is housed partly in buildings dating back to the 16th century, on the site of the Chapel of St Ayles (built by the Monks of Balmerino Abbey in the 12th century). The most recent buildings were added in 1996, providing room for additional displays.

A fishing lugger in Anstruther Harbour

The *Reaper* is a 'Fifie' herring lugger – the Fifie was the most popular model of drifter on the East Coast in the 19th and early 20th centuries.

B **Isle of May:** St Adrian landed there around 800 AD and subsequently built a monastery. The first of the island's three lighthouses was built by John Cunninghame in 1636. Trips to the island – which is now a bird sanctuary – run from the harbour. Check details at the kiosk.

C **Cellardyke Town Hall:** Built in 1883 (the original hall was built in 1624). The remains of the Market Cross, erected in 1642, are fixed to the wall.

Cellardyke Town Hall

The Market Cross

Walk 5 (continued)

D **Architecture:** Two cottages on the right with typical East Neuk features: pantiled roofs, crowstepped gables and forestairs, enabling the upstairs to be accessed directly from the street.

On the left is a good example of a marriage lintel, showing the date and initials of the resident couple: 1709, TS and MD

E **Cellardyke Harbour:** Dating from the 16th century, and nowadays only used for yachts, the harbour is said to have acquired its name from the cellars cut in the hillside, where the fishermen stored their nets.

Cellardyke Harbour

F **Johnstone Lodge:** The current building (1829) stands on the site of a house built by a local magistrate around 1690. In 1708 the 'Old Pretender' was supposed to have met his supporters there in secret. Titaua Marama, a Tahitian Princess who married a local man in 1878, lived here for twenty years. She is buried in St Adrian's Churchyard.

G **Melville's Manse:** Built in 1590 for James Melville, the local minister. In 1587 a Spanish galleon from the Armada put in to Anstruther after being shipwrecked. Melville advised that the crew should be treated kindly and later they were allowed to sail back to Spain. There is no public access.

H **St Adrian's Church:** Dates from the mid 17th century. The grave stones are the main interest.

St Adrian's Church

I **Old Post Office Close:** Thomas Chalmers (1780-1847) was born here. He studied at St Andrews University and became professor of Theology at Edinburgh before becoming the first Moderator of the breakaway United Free Church in 1843. He was a great orator and was also responsible for building the lighthouse at the end of the pier.

J **Anstruther Wester Church:** Now a hall. The steeple was built in the 16th century (originally used as a prison). Some interesting grave stones, including one in the shape of a coffin – reputed to be that of St Adrian, and to have floated over from the Isle of May in 873.

K **Buckie House:** Built in the 1690s. In the 19th century Alexander Bachelor, a slater, covered the house, including some of the interior, with shells and charged people to view it.

Buckie House

The house is now owned by the National Trust for Scotland.

L **Wightmans Wynd:** Named after a smuggler who pretended his house was haunted by a black lady to cover his smuggling activities.

M **Dreel House:** Site of Dreel Castle, one time home of the Anstruther family, which dated back to the 13th century.

Wightmans Wynd

Walk 6: *Falkland*

Dating back to the 14th century, Falkland is tiny but highly picturesque. It is home to Scotland's only royal hunting lodge, Falkland Palace, which has been fully restored and is open to the public along with its fine gardens.

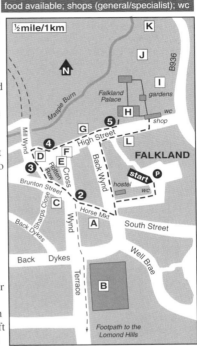

food available; shops (general/specialist); wc

Start from the car park in the centre of the village (follow signs up Back Wynd from the High St). Walk out of the main entrance to the car park and turn left, up Back Wynd, then first right along Horse Market (A) to the junction with Cross Wynd.

2 A diversion to the left at this point will lead uphill to a point of access to the Lomond Hills, passing St John's Works (B), a huge red brick factory, on your left. For this route, however, cross the road and continue along Brunton Street, with Brunton House (C) on your left and a pleasant open space on your right. When you reach the Cottage Craft Centre look left up Sharps Close, with its fine row of weavers' cottages, before turning right down a cobbled lane (Rotten Row).

3 At the foot of the lane cross the High Street and go on down Mill Wynd beyond. Turn right immediately after the Stag Inn (D), up what appears to be a dead end close, and climb a flight of steps leading into the Square.

4 To your right, in the corner of the Square, is Cameron House (E). Turn left and walk along the near side of the Square. The distinctive Bruce Fountain (F) with its red lions is on your right, and the statue of Onesiphorus Bruce (also F) in the grounds of the Parish Church on your left. Continue past Maspie House (G), to reach the main entrance to the Palace (H). A tour round the Palace will be the highlight of any visit to the village – you can choose to visit it now or at the end of your walk. There is an entry fee to the Palace, but entrance to the garden is free (I, J, K).

5 If you are not visiting the Palace, walk past the Gatehouse and continue as far as the National Trust Shop (also providing access to the garden). Cross the street and turn right. Immediately opposite the main entrance to the Palace, is Moncrief House (L), with the Hunting Lodge Hotel next door. Beyond the bank, turn left up Back Wynd to return to the car park.

Walk 6 (continued)

[A] **Horse Market:** Probably the site of one of the regular fairs held in the town. On your right is a good example of a forestair.

A forestair

[B] **St John's Works:** The linen industry was important to Falkland from the Middle Ages. At that time flax was grown locally. Later it was imported, and by 1870 the first power loom was installed in St John's Works, which later produced linoleum and now packaging.

[C] **Brunton House:** Built in 1712, this was the home of the Simson family – hereditary falconers to the crown.

[D] **Stag Inn:** Built in 1680 (note the marriage lintel). This is an example of the restoration carried out in the Falkland Conservation Area: the first such area to be designated in Scotland.

[E] **Cameron House:** Birth place of Richard Cameron in 1648. Known as the 'Lion of the Covenant', he was an Episcopalian and a school master, but joined the Covenanters and died at Airds Moss in 1680, fighting to depose Charles II.

Cameron House

Bruce Fountain

[F] **Bruce Fountain and Statue of Onesiphorus Tyndall Bruce:** In 1820 Professor Bruce bought Falkland Palace, together with the Keepership of the Palace. His niece Margaret inherited the office. She married Onesiphorus Tyndall, an English barrister. They built Falkland House, which lies to the west of the town, as the Palace was a semi-ruin.

[G] **Maspie House:** Home of G Deas, Lord of Session in the 19th century. Now a gift shop. The spiral stair leads down into the shop, through which you can gain access to the attractive garden at the back with a view of the Palace orchard.

[H] **Falkland Palace:** The Palace was first used as a royal hunting lodge by James II (reigned 1437-60) and remained a favourite residence of subsequent Stewart monarchs, including Mary, Queen of Scots and James VI & I. The layout of the building as it appears today was largely the work of James IV (1488-1513) and, above all, James V (1513-1542), who employed continental and Scottish masons to turn the Palace into one of the finest Renaissance buildings in Scotland.

The building was little used after James VI became king of both Scotland and England (following the Union of the Crowns in 1603), and fell largely into disrepair after Cromwell's soldiers caused a fire in the east wing in 1654. During the Jacobite rebellion of 1715, the Palace was briefly garrisoned by a party of MacGregors, amongst whom was the infamous Rob Roy.

In 1887 John Crichton Stuart, 3rd Marquis of Bute, bought the title of Hereditary Keeper and set about restoring the Palace. The work was finally completed by his grandson, Michael Crichton Stuart, who moved into the Palace in 1946. In 1952 he made the National Trust for Scotland the Deputy Keeper of the Palace.

The interior of the Palace is simultaneously sumptuous and homely; its small rooms illuminated by bright wall hangings and tapestries, painted ceilings, heraldic displays and numerous portraits of the Stewart monarchs

Walk 6 (continued)

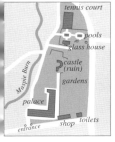

Falkland Palace

of the 16th and 17th centuries.

Having looked round the Palace, do not forget to explore the gardens (*see* below).

Details of the Palace and its grounds can be found in the very comprehensive guide book provided by the Trust. There are also guided tours.

I Palace Garden: There has always been a garden at Falkland, but following the loss of the Palace's royal residents it went onto decline. During the First and Second World Wars the garden was dug up; being used as a forestry nursery in the first war and for growing potatoes in the second. In 1946 Percy Cane, a leading English garden architect, was commissioned to design a new garden within the existing boundaries. The current garden is relaxed and informal, with wide lawns and long borders, ponds, a small glasshouse and the worn stone walls of the old tennis court (*see* K).

J The Castle: The remains of the tower of the original castle, dating from the 12th century. This was owned by the McDuff Earls of Fife – the owners of the site before it was obtained by James I.

K Royal Tennis Court: The game of Royal (or Real) Tennis ('Court Tennis' in the USA) is the more complicated ancestor of Lawn Tennis (which dates from no earlier than the 1860s-70s). This particular court was built for James V in 1539, making it the oldest in Britain. In addition, it is Britain's only remaining *court quarré* (ie, it has penthouses on only two sides of the court instead of the now typical three). It is also odd amongst other surviving courts in being without a roof.

Royal Tennis Court

There is a group in Falkland who play on the court regularly. (The various facets of the game are explained in a video and exhibition in a former changing room).

Lettering on panel on Moncrief House

L Moncrief House: Built in 1610 for one of James VI's courtiers. Note the thatched roof and the gilded lettering above the door and on the panel to the right. The neighbouring Hunting Lodge Hotel dates from 1607.

Other Towns & Villages (see map on p18)

Pittenweem
`food available; shops (general/specialist); wc`

The town of Pittenweem is clustered around a picturesque harbour, home to a fleet of commercial fishing boats. The heart of the harbour is the large modern fish market, which helps to maintain the town's position as the busiest of the East Fife ports today. Fish is sold

Harbour and Fish Market

Entrance to St Fillan's Cave

early in the morning at the market. A broad street of attractive buildings frames the harbour. The centre of town can be reached by a walk up a number of extremely attractive lanes.

The 'weem' part of Pittenweem comes from the gaelic word for 'cave' – a reference to St Fillan's Cave (situated just behind the harbour and open to the public), believed to have been inhabited by an early Christian missionary.

St Monans
`food available; shops (limited); wc`

An attractive village with fishermens' houses clustered round a small harbour. The town is best known today for the 14th-century kirk on a hill to the south of the harbour; its stubby steeple a well-known local landmark. On the coast to the north is a windmill built in the 18th century to pump seawater into salt pans (open to

St Monans Parish Church

the public for a short period during the summer – check dates locally).

Elie & Earlsferry
`food available; shops (general); wc`

Unlike their northern neighbours, the connected villages of Elie and Earlsferry have an expansive feel, with the well spaced buildings set back from the sandy beach as it sweeps in a broad curve protected on each end by low rocky outcrops. Here there is more of an emphasis on leisure, with many pleasure craft and opportunities

Earlsferry from Elie Harbour

for visitors to enjoy a variety of watersports.

Other Towns & Villages (continued)

Lower Largo

`food available; shops (general); wc`

The most southerly of the small coastal villages of the East Neuk, Lower Largo has some charming examples of old fishermens' cottages. The village is joined to Lundin Links to the south west, with its fine links golf courses.

Harbour at Lower Largo

The village's most famous son was Alexander Selkirk (1676-1728): a seaman who was marooned on a deserted island for four years, and whose experiences were the basis for Defoe's *Robinson Crusoe*. There is a small statue of Selkirk above the door of his birthplace.

Cupar

`food available; shops (general/specialist); wc`

Cupar, in the midst of the farmland of the Howe of Fife, is a substantial town with a long history. Its records go back to the 13th century and it remained the county town of Fife until 1976, when the Council moved its headquarters to Glenrothes. The closure of the agricultural market, in 1994, was a further blow to the town's ancient prestige, but the Mercat Cross still stands proud in the centre of town, and Cupar still retains a role as the busy administrative centre for North East Fife, with a wide array of shops and services. There are also many leisure facilities for visitors to enjoy.

The Market Cross

Ceres

`food available; shops (general/specialist); wc`

A small, picturesque village dating back to the 14th century, built around a village green. Formerly a centre for agriculture and weaving, the village is now home to the Fife Folk Museum and The Griselda Pottery, well known for its revival of Weymss Ware. Within walking distance are Hill of Tarvit House

The Provost

(National Trust for Scotland) and Scotstarvit Tower, both good examples of laird's residences from different eras (*See* p32).

Fife Folk Museum

Visitor Attractions & Activities

St Andrews

Museums, Galleries & Attractions

St Andrews Aquarium (F2, Walk 1)
An exhibition of many species of marine life, both native and tropical, down by the shore in St Andrews. Limited disabled access.
◆ ⌑ S £ WC

British Golf Museum (E2, Walk 1)
The comprehensive history of golf with pictures and commentary – a must for golf enthusiasts. Disabled access.
◇ S £ WC

Crawford Arts Centre (F3, Walk 1)
Art galleries with changing exhibitions, plus a studio theatre which stages university and local productions. Disabled access.
◆ S *FREE* WC (not disabled)

St Andrews Museum (D4)
Sited in Kinburn house, built for Buddo Family in 1854, the museum explores the history of St Andrews from medieval times to the present a day. Disabled access.
◆ ⌑ S *FREE* WC

St Andrews Preservation Trust Museum (G4, Walk 2)
Charming traditional building carrying exhibits relating to St Andrews' history – displays of old St Andrews shops, photographs and other memorabilia – plus a pleasant garden to rest in.
◇ *FREE*

Historic Buildings & Gardens

St Andrews Botanic Garden (D6, Walk 3)
An 18 acre garden, including glasshouse, with many rare and beautiful plants. Disabled access (it is possible to hire a wheelchair). Some plants on sale.
◆ ⌑ £ WC

St Andrews Castle & Visitor Centre (G3, Walk 2)
A fine old ruin, plus a Visitor Centre detailing the history of the Castle, starting with the bringing of St Andrew's relics to Kilrimont in the 700s. Good range of books on St Andrews and Scottish history in the shop. Limited disabled access. (A joint ticket for entry to both the Castle and Cathedral is available at both.)
◆ S £ WC

St Andrews Cathedral (H4, Walk 2)
The ruins of the Cathedral, plus the free-standing St Rule's Tower and a visitor centre in the Warming House and Undercroft – all that remains of the Priory. The most important exhibit is the Sarcophagus of St Andrew, one of the finest examples of Dark Age Art (ca. 800 AD). Also, the remains of tombstones dated between 1300-1700 and the seals of the bishops and priors. Disabled access to the Museum but not to the shop. (A joint ticket for entry to both the Castle and Cathedral is available at both.)
◆ S £

Visitor Attractions & Activities (continued)

Theatre & Cinema

The Byre Theatre of St Andrews (G4)
Abbey Street (*tel.* 01334 475000)
A new, custom-built theatre opened in 2001, on the site of the old theatre. It has two auditoriums and there are performances throughout the year. Disabled access.
◆ ⌶ £ WC

New Picture House (cinema)
North Street (*tel.* 01334 473509)

Sports & Leisure

Golf
St Andrews Links Trust *(tel 01334 466666)* operates 6 courses in the town, which are open to the public seven days per week (except for the Old Course, which closes on Sunday).

The Old Course requires proof of handicap from non-members. Advance Booking is essential, though there is also a daily ballot for the Old Course.

The Eden, Jubilee, Strathtyrum and Balgove Courses require you to book 24 hours in advance or take your chance and just turn up on the day.

East Sands Leisure Centre (I7)
Behind East Sands
Swimming pool; sauna; squash, snooker and table tennis. Disabled access.
◆ ⌶ £ WC

Walking
There is a footpath leading east along the coast from East Sands, and another leading to Cambo from the end of Walk 3. For details of these and other walks in Fife, see the companion volume to this guide, *Walks Fife* (£2.50), or one of the other guide books available locally.

East Fife

Museums & Attractions

Crail Museum & Heritage Centre (Walk 4)
The history of Crail and the surrounding area.
◇ 🅂 *FREE*

Fife Folk Museum
Ceres (see map on p18)
In the heart of the pretty village of Ceres, this museum explains the history of rural Fife.
◇ 🅂 £

Scottish Deer Centre
Two miles west of Cupar on A91
Many species of deer, falconry, shops, play parks and much more.
◆ ⌶ 🅂 £ WC

Visitor Attractions & Activities (continued)

Scottish Fisheries Museum (Walk 5)
Anstruther
A must for anyone interested in boats or the sea. Models, paintings, boats and other exhibits covering all aspects of Scotland's fishing industry past and present.
◆ ⊔ S £ WC

Historic Buildings & Gardens
Falkland Palace (Walk 6)
A superb historic royal hunting lodge dating from the 15th-16th centuries – one of the finest Renaissance buildings in Scotland. Also a splendid formal garden.
◇ S £ WC

Hill of Tarvit House & Scotstarvit Tower
Two miles south of Cupar on A916
Hill of Tarvit is a National Trust for Scotland property: an Edwardian mansion containing fine displays of paintings and furniture set in a pleasant garden. A key is also available for those wishing to visit the nearby Scotstarvit Tower: a fine 17th-century tower house.
◇ ⊔ £ WC

Kellie Castle
Seven miles west of Crail on the B9171
A splendid old castle (14th century onwards, restored in the late 19th century), now owned by the National Trust for Scotland. Fine walled garden.
◇ ⊔ S £ WC

Scotland's Secret Bunker
Three miles west of Crail on the B940
An underground labyrinth of reinforced concrete intended to house the British government had atomic war broken out.
◇ ⊔ S £ WC

Sports & Leisure
Boat Trips
Throughout the summer there is a daily boat trip from Anstruther out to the Isle of May: a wildlife sanctuary in the Firth of Forth inhabited by puffins, grey seals and much more.

Golf
There are over 40 (and rising) golf courses in Fife, ranging from the highest championship level to 9-holers. Check with Tourist Information Centres (*see* back cover) for the nearest courses and how to book a round.

Walking
Eastern Fife has some splendid walking, including the coast walks of the Fife Coastal Path and the hill walks in the Lomond Hills south of Falkland (*see* Walk 6).

For details of routes throughout Fife, consult *Walks Fife* (£2.50), the companion volume to this guide.